BURN AFTER READING

poems

JESSICA CIENCIN HENRIQUEZ

Rev Publishing

New York | Los Angeles | Paris | Bogotá

Rev Publishing
New York | Los Angeles | Paris | Bogotá
www.rev-publishing.com

Printed in Colombia

ISBN: 979-8-9915794-9-0 (hardcover)
ISBN: 979-8-9915794-8-3 (ebook)
ISBN: 979-8-9915794-1-4 (audiobook)

Library of Congress Control Number: 2024919890

Author's Note

To understand how this book was born, you need to understand what first had to die.

I've been writing my whole life—first to survive, then to prove I was worthy of surviving. Before this book was written, I had spent five years writing a memoir, pain turned into 280 pages. I bled every word into those chapters. But five years is a long time for a story to stay stagnant. By the time the manuscript was ready to be published, I had changed. I outgrew the narrative that life was pain, that love was unfair, that healing was only for those who had suffered enough. I was no longer the woman who wrote it.

I turned to a ritual I've done many times in my life, something known throughout South America as a Despacho. This fire ceremony is a long-held tradition to honor transitions, to give thanks, and to let go. It's incredibly simple but the impact is profound. I gathered together an offering of flowers, grains, sugar, and leaves. Each element carrying its own significance; sugar symbolizes the sweetness and the pleasure of life, flowers to honor both beauty and impermanence; grains for abundance, and leaves placed with intention.

I bundled my book together with the gifts, lit the match, and closed my eyes as it all began to burn.

How can I explain what it feels like to mourn something that has never fully come to life? Maybe I don't have to. Maybe you already know.

I slowly opened my eyes, watching as the fire devoured the petals and my pages, each one curling inwards, the edges blackening and turning to gray, slowly transforming history into ash. I thought I would feel relief, but instead, I felt a wave of panic.

What if I never wrote again?
What if I had nothing left to say?
Who would I be if I wasn't a writer?

I watched the fire rise and then rest, slowly dying down. Soon, I felt a sense of quiet and then the weightlessness that comes with surrender. I didn't have answers to those questions, but I was willing to wait, and find out.

The next morning, when I knelt over the fire pit to clear the ashes,I found something that, to this day, I can't explain.

There, buried under blackened pages, one folded fragment survived, its edges charred but a few scattered words still visible:

> "what   truth   remains"

If I hadn't seen this for myself, I'd never have believed it. My sensibility could never accept that the universe would ever be so obvious. But I did see it. And when I did, I smiled at the absurdity, and then at the audacity. For me, this moment was clear, a divine invitation: keep writing, but write the truth."

This book in your hands is my promise—to do only that.

Noah Rev—
how lucky we are
to walk this earth together
again and again and again.

. . .

IGNITE

Create Her

Don't you dare say you don't know how,
don't know if you can,
don't know if you're strong enough.
Look around you—

Can't you see what your hands have made?
Can't you see what you have breathed into being?
Can't you see the lifetimes you have laid down
to begin this one?

When will you learn how to awaken your ancestors?
When will you learn how to summon them by name?
When will you learn their power is yours to invoke?
Divinity has been showing herself all this time—

yet when you look into your own eyes,
you stare right past her,
seeing only the creation,
and not the creator.

Create Her

Don't you dare say you don't know how,
don't know if you can,
don't know if you're strong enough.
Look around you--

Can't you see what your hands have made?
Can't you see what you have breathed into being?
Can't you see the lifetimes you have laid down
to begin this one?

When will you learn how to awaken your ancestors?
When will you learn how to summon them by name?
When will you learn their power is yours to invoke?
Divinity has been showing herself all this time--

yet when you look into your own eyes,
you stare right past her,
seeing only the creation,
and not the creator.

First Breath

Breach, backward, the cord around her neck—
she is cut from her mother
who was cut from her mother
who was the final cut of her mother's life.

There is a violence in birth—
none of us remembers
being pried from one body
and thrust into this one.

What matters here is often forgotten—
the karma, the cleansing, the redemption.
This existence resets with a rush of blood,
purpling skin, a gasp, a cry, a breath of beginning.

Why would we choose this?
Why did we choose this?
Why will we choose this again?

We come into this world with nothing
but the seven sins of our fathers,
laid against the supple skin of our mothers.
We drink life from the living.

We arrive defenseless,
unprotected creatures
and yet we decided all of this,
down to the name.

We are making a future
and it will cost us our past,
all we experience here
will not, cannot last.

These stories
we are writing
were never meant
to be the measure of us

but supposed to teach us,
to un-breach us, to upright us,
to untie the cords from around our necks,
readying us for the next first breath.

First Breath

Breach, backward, the cord around her neck—
she is cut from her mother
who was cut from her mother
who was the final cut of her mother's life.

There is a violence in birth—
none of us remembers
being pried from one body
and thrust into **this** one.

What **matters** here is often forgotten—
the karma, the cleansing, the redemption.
This existence resets with a rush of blood,
purpling skin, a gasp, a cry, a breath of beginning.

Why would we choose this?
Why did we choose this?
Why will we choose this again?

We come into this world with **not**hing
but the s**even** sins of our fathers,
laid against the supple skin of **our** mothers.
We drink life from the living.

We arrive defenseless,
unprotected creatures
and yet we decided all of this,
d**own** to the **name.**

We are making a future
and **it** will cost us our past,
all we experience here
will not, cannot last.

These stories
we are writing
were never meant
to be the measure of us

but s**up**posed to teach us,
to un-breach us, to upright us,
to untie the cords from around our necks,
readying us for the next first breath.

Remembering

If our mothers
gave us the name

G O D

Would we still
forget who we are?

Or would we see our own hands
the way we see stars—
as light not borrowed
but belonging to us?

If our fathers
gave us the name

G A I A

would we still
forget what we have made?

Or would we remember
that we are still shaping
this earth?

Passing By

Lilacs don't know
                        whether they are

o   g
      p   n
            e   n   i

or closing,

whether their petals
are f
          a
              l
                  l
                        i
                            n
                                g
                                  toward the earth.

They don't know
who they are,
but they know
spirit is using them
to pour joy
into every person
passing by.

Safety

At some point we'll stop
hovering our hands
over our babies' bellies
and trust
that what we brought to life
will go on living without
our worry or our witness
without our guiding or deciding
what must happen toward the end

Let us keep our fears quiet
so our children do not become fluent
in a language we hope to extinct
let them emerge out of
life's tender cocoon
ready and ready and ready
to find their own safety
in this world we've made for them
in this world we've tried
to keep them from

Safety

At some point we'll stop
hovering our hands
over our babies' bellies
and trust
that what we brought to life
will go on living without
our worry or our witness
without our guiding or deciding
what must happen toward the end

Let us keep our fears quiet
so our children do not become fluent
in a language we hope to extinct
let them emerge out of
life's tender cocoon
ready and ready and ready
to find their own safety
in this world we've made for them
in this world we've tried
to keep them from

Cage

When you say cage, I think of rib,
think of Adam, think of Eve.
I think of how she was conceived,
made after man
not before yet her name implies
there is something more to come.

I think of her sons,
think of their birth, marking the start
of suffering on earth,
marking the end of innocence.
Though, in a sense, that loss came
as Adam swallowed the apple.

I think of what followed after
the inception of sin:
Punishment and blame and lying.
I think of lashing and penance and pain.
I think of what could be, could have been.
When you say men, I think of cage.

Cage

When **you say** cage, **I** think of rib,
think of Adam, think of Eve.
I think of how she **was** conceived,
made after man
not be**for**e yet her name implies
there is **something more** to come.

I think of her sons,
think of their birth, marking the start
of suffering on earth,
marking the end of innocence.
Though, in a sense, that loss came
as Adam sw**allow**ed the apple.

I think of what followed after
the inception of sin:
Punish**me**nt and blame and lying.
I think of lashing and penance and pain.
I think of wha**t** c**ou**ld **be**, could have been.
When you say men, **I** think of cage.

Coming For Herself

How can you ask
for more than a sunset,
a daily miracle
you don't bother to witness?

Each evening she arrives, on time,
more beautiful than before,
painting red brushstrokes against heaven's floor
like the burning cheeks of a child after too much play.

She lights the sky with chaos in her hues
of crimson, gold, and lavender bruises,
echoing Tzigane's fire when the violins lose control
but you have long stopped listening to her music.

She is waiting, and still, you turn your back on her colors
as if there is anything in this world
worthier of your attention.
She lowers herself into the earth as she goes ignored.

She used to come for you, but now she knows
what we will all at some point learn:
there is no one else— If she decides to come tomorrow,
she is only coming for herself.

Coming For Herself

How can you ask
for more than a sunset,
a daily miracle
you don't bother to witness?

Each evening she arrives, on time,
more beautiful than before,
painting red brushstrokes against heaven's floor
like the burning cheeks of a child after too much play.

She lights the sky with chaos in her hues
of crimson, gold, and lavender bruises,
echoing Tzigane's fire when the violins lose control
but you have long stopped listening to her music.

She is waiting, and still, you turn your back on her colors
as if there is anything in this world
worthier of your attention.
She lowers herself into the earth as she goes ignored.

She used to come for you, but now she knows
what we will all at some point learn:
there is no one else— If she decides to come tomorrow,
she is only coming for herself.

Her Majesty

Do you remember
the first time you saw the sea?
I don't mean as a child
on hands and knees shoveling
sand into a mouth with no teeth,
all gum and giggle and hunger.
while the tide licks away
the drip castles you're learning to create.

I mean the first time your eyes
were peeled with purity
as you stood in silent awe
of the power she holds in each wave,
as she calmly roars and reaches
toward the sky,
tempted to touch something
mightier than herself.

I mean the first time you saw
how she gracefully rolls treasures
and bones to your feet,
an offering of sand-dollars and shark teeth,
death or life arriving in relentless rhythm.
Neither ever leaves her shores willingly.
She waits with wonder to see
which you'll choose
which you value most.

Do you remember
the first time you bowed
to the ways she rebels?
As she cascades over the shoreline,
tasting concrete, rolling trees,
drowning buildings that will never be rebuilt?
How could a creature be so tender
and in the same caress, cause destruction?

I remember the first time I saw the sea—
I cried, I asked how, how, how
could we ever want more than this?
She called me in and swept me up safely,
salt gracing my mouth, my lips,
healing every wound but not without burning,
she reminded me of what I already knew—
There is nothing more than her majesty.

Her Majesty

Do you **remember**
the first time you saw the sea?
I don't mean as a child
on hands and knees shoveling
sand into a mouth with no teeth,
all gum and giggle and hunger,
while the tide licks away
the drip castles **you're learning** to create.

I mean the first time your eyes
were peeled **with** purity
as you stood in silent awe
of the power she holds in each wave,
as you stood in silent awe
of the power she holds in **each** wave,
as she calmly, roars and reaches
toward the sky.

I mean the first time you saw
how she gracefully rolls treasures
and bones to your feet,
an offering of sand-dollars and shark teeth,
death or **life** arriving in relentless rhythm.
Neither ever leaves her shores willingly.
She waits with wonder to see
which **you'll** choose
which you value most.

Do you remember
the first time you bowed
to the ways she rebels?
As she cascades over the shoreline,
tastes concrete, rolls trees,
drowns buildings that will never be rebuilt?
How could a creature be so tender
and in the same caress, cause destruction?

I remember the first time I saw the sea—
I cried, I asked how, how, how
could we ever want more than this?
She called me in and swept me up safely,
salt gracing my mouth, my lips,
healing every wound but not without burning,
she reminded me of what I already knew—
There is nothing more than her majesty.

Chorus

Every Monday at 9 am
I meet with the other goddesses
just past the orange grove.
We drop our shoes at the door,
and tuck our socks and egos inside,
before we find our places
in the moon valley.
Facing one another,
with mugs warming palms,
limbs long, we slowly slip awake.

Mourning doves circle,
their wings outstretched
against the softness of the rug.
Sparrows sit perched
beside the fire, readying,
and readying, and readying.
The nightingales land
where their melodies
are needed most.

And with our hands conducting,
we reach down our throats,
and into our bellies,
to pull out the voices
the world has pushed down.

With wisdom we chant,
weave white magic
back into our beautiful bodies—
bodies of mothers,
bodies of lovers,
bodies of givers and creators,
and conquerors and queens.

Our wild, wild winds
reshape the silence,
uncoiling from within us
ribbons of light.

We count from five,
and together recover
what has been lost—
taken, forgotten,
or tossed away before
we knew the worth of exactly what
we held in our hands.

This is our feeding hour,
when each soul is satiated.
We stitch up in one another
what the world has wind-torn,
and feeling reborn, we stand.

We pluck our socks
from our shoes,
drape our egos
loosely around our necks,
and fly out the door
over the grove—
back to our nests
to reverberate this remembrance,
this rite, this rebellion,
throughout the rest of our lives.

No Mistakes

I never saw my mother diet,
or cleanse, or cinch, or fast,
never saw her standing
in front of a mirror,
lifting her breasts,
letting them fall.

I never saw her
pushing food around her plate
until it blended
into something that looked
mostly eaten.

I never saw her grab
at the flesh of her belly,
demanding to know,
where did this come from?

I never saw her layering
under baggy clothes
to hide from men,
or pouring into tight dresses
to be noticed by them.

These are things
I learned from women
who were not my mother.

They taught me
the language to degrade
our bodies,
in public and in private:

Fat ass.
     Flat ass.
          Gordita.
            Flaquita.
      Big boned.
   Thunder thighs.
 Plus-sized.
Scrawny.

I despised the dialogue
given by these women,
apologetic, as if existing was a sin.
They swallowed the guilt
for consuming more than the minimum
required to sustain them.

I watched as they peeled off clothes
leaving patterns on their skin,
full moon dents where
buttons had been,
stitches tracked along their thighs.

I dreaded the camaraderie
that came from sharing
in this social self-hatred.

I wish I had your legs,
mine are so short.
I wish I had your hair,
mine is so dry,
I wish I had your hips,
mine are so wide.
I wish, I wish, I wish…

I wish my mother's voice
had a microphone
to drown out the noise
from the women
who did not raise me.

When the world
insisted I look different,
I heard her song in my head,
reminding me of how beautiful I was
not because of the way I looked
but because of who made me.
And She makes no mistakes.

Space

I will let you
peek into your life
ten years from today.

For just one moment,
take a long look around.

See what you've made.
See what you've become.
See how much love exists
in   this   space.

ILLUMINATE

Home

You placed your hand
on the soft of my belly,
and I cradled that breath
for the rest of eternity.

How was it
that your fingerprints were
already there, indelibly etched
by other lifetimes?

My stomach, ancient earth, stone walls,
our history drawn
in lines, ridges,
and the creases of your palm.

You spent half a century
finding your way back to us,
to the bed you'd once made
 in my body.

I didn't know the details of you then,
but I knew touch
like that
doesn't happen twice.

You kept your hand
where it belonged
as the sun wove itself
into the earth.

I wanted to tell you
about the fear I'd held there,
in this place no longer
than the length from wrist to fingertip.

We sat instead in silence,
communicating as the pando does
through one root, a quiet conversation
beneath the forest floor.

This was the beginning of us,
you understanding
every word
I left unsaid.

I put my hand
on top of yours,
kept the other
pressed still on my heart,

This is how I calmed myself
without you.
This is how I carried myself
toward you.

These two touch-points
have been my compass,
until that afternoon, until you,
until I knew

this is the direction
I am going—
we are going
home.

Home

You placed your hand

on the soft of my belly,
and I cradled that breath
for the rest of eternity.

How was it
that your fingerprints were
already there, indelibly **etched**
by other lifetimes?

My stomach, ancient earth, stone w**all**s,
our history drawn
in lines, ridges,
and the creases **of your** palm.

You spent half a century
finding your way back to us,
to the bed you'd once made
in my body.

I didn't know the details of you then,
but I knew touch
like that
doesn't happen twice.

You kept your hand
where it belonged
as the sun wove itself
into the earth.

I wanted to tell you
about the **fear** I'd long held there,
in this place no l**on**ger
than the length from wrist **to** fingertip.

We sat instead in silence,
communicating as the pando does
through one root, a quiet conversation
beneath the forest floor.

This was the beginning of us,
you understanding
every word
I left un**said**

I put my h**and**
on top of yours,
kept the other
pressed **still** on my heart,

This is how **I calme**d myself
without you.
This is how I carried myself
toward you.

These two touch-points
have been my compass,
until that afternoon, until you,
until I knew

this is the direction
I am going—
we are going
home.

Heart Open

Go into the garden,
with bare feet,
sit under
the pepper trees,
listen to the music
the winds play
for only you.

Find words to sing along
with the song
you're composing together
as yesterday's rain rushes
down the mountain
ready for his solo.

Pick a pomegranate,
let your fingernails rip
into ripe crimson skin.

Feel each seed burst
between your teeth,
swallow sweet
drop by drop.

Watch as the hawk circles
blessing you by landing
on the branch beside you.

Don't move.

Breathe in slowly
this moment.
There is nowhere else
you need to be.

No one else
needs you more
than the hawk,
and the river
and the music
and the mountain
need your attention.

And now tell us the truth—
can you remember
what was just about
to break your heart open?

Yours

the moment you step outside
and the sun hits your naked shoulders
the first soothing swallow of soup
when you're sick
the sand between bed sheets
the yawn you caught from someone you love
the color you see before sight comes
the hot red sun setting on the Mediterranean sea
the feeling of sinking into your seat when we take off
the monsoon sky just before she is about to collapse
the first breath of oxygen after the drop-off
when the sea shelf disappears
from beneath your feet
the free fall without a parachute
heading toward certain destiny
with a smile on my face
that is how it feels
to be yours

Enough

Why do you go inside
when it rains?
Enough. Enough.
Abandon your umbrellas,
surrender your shoes.
Thunder is your
two minute warning.
Get up, get out—
stand under the sky
let her open her arms to you.
Watch the way
children play with her—
spinning in circles,
eyes closed, arms wide.

Mimic their freedom
until it becomes yours.
Get wet, get dirty, get dizzy—
get to the good part,
the part you've forgotten.

Why don't you rush outside
when it rains?
Lift your chin, open your mouth—
drink in every drop.
Let what nourishes the trees,
what cleanses the earth,
do her work in you.

Sight

Revealing how soft
a man can be
before he's ever felt
the honey of
his own tenderness
is like that moment
in every movie
when they pluck
the glasses
from a stunning
woman's face
as though her beauty
was not already obvious
to the rare ones with sight

Sight

Revealing how soft
a man can be
before he's ever felt
the honey of
his own **tenderness**
is **like** that moment
in every movie
when they pluck
the glasses
from a stunning
woman's face
as though her beauty
was not already obv**i**ou**s**
to the **rare** ones with sight

Why Not

You are getting older now.
I notice how you don't ask
to stop at the playground
as we pass by on the way home
how you're shouting for mom!
instead of *mama, wait, mama, come back!*
how what used to be play dates
are now called hang-outs.

I hate hate hate
that we aren't kids at the same time.
In this life, you are the child
and I am the grown-up.
while you flip off the diving board,
I must talk to other dry parents
about how long it takes
to get permits for pools
they'll never midnight-swim in.

You make sandcastles
but I pack apples and reapply sunblock.
You come home covered in dirt
and I demand you take a shower,
brush your teeth, get ready for bed.
You grew up too soon,
and I missed it. I miss it.
I'm missing it now as I write these words
and you are outside the kitchen window
filling up water balloons because
you still live in a world of why not.

Why Not

You are **getting older** now.
I notice how you don't ask
to stop at the playground
as we pass by on the way home
how you're shouting for mom
instead of *mama, wait, mama, come back!*
how what used to be play dates
are now called hang-outs.

I hate hate hate
that we aren't kids at the same time.
In this **life, you** are the child
 and I am the grown-up.
while you flip off the diving board,
I must talk to other dry parents
about how long it takes
to get permits for pools
they'll never midnight-swim in.

You make sandcastles
but I pack apples and reapply sunblock.
You come home covered in dirt
and I demand you take a shower,
brush your teeth, get ready for bed.
You grew up too **soon,**
and **I** missed it. **I miss** it.
I'm missing it now as I write these words
and you are outside the kitchen window
 filling up water balloons because
you still live in a world of why not.

Undone

You make love to me all day,
in a thousand ways,
I never knew one person
could make love to another.

With one hand
on the steering wheel
and the other
caressing the back of my neck.

When you pull over
to listen to the story I'm telling,
so you can look me in the eyes
and cry at all the right parts.

When you run our bath,
and warm my tea,
and show me every single day
how you worship my body.

When you rest your head
against my heart,
inviting me to know
a tenderness I have never met.

When we sleep,
and you wrap yourself around me,
as if your limbs are dying to say:
I'm here, I'm here, I'm here.

For much of this life,
I thought love was a taking thing,
but here you are,
giving and giving and giving.

Before you, I feared gentle touch,
believing I would turn to dust
and scatter with the breeze—
that's how brittle I'd become.

But here I am,
wholly undone in front of you.
Please, don't stop
loving me back to life.

When She Goes

You ask what I did today,
and I tell you I watched a butterfly.
"That's it?" you ask.
"That's a lot," I say.

With one tilt of your head, I know
you've never spent your time this way—
not minutes, not hours,
not entire afternoons.

A therapist once asked me to write a list
of what I'd like to accomplish in life.
She handed me a pen and a page, and I returned
one line, a single sentence touched with truth:

I want to be so still
that a butterfly lands on my skin.

She gave me the look you're giving me now,
a look that knows a life of crowded sidewalks
and impatiently ticking clocks, a look that says:
What about money, what about work,
what about legacy, what about things that matter?

But I don't understand what could matter more
than the serious business of watching butterflies.
What could please a person
more than this?

Being still and doing nothing are not the same.
Most people excel at doing nothing.
They waste minutes, hours, entire afternoons
tasting all the flavors of nothingness.

They build an identity around the well of it.
They fill their days with the noise of nothing,
calling it life, calling it love,
calling it purpose.

But to be still is to be devoured by a moment,
to learn to turn to statue
when you are desperate to reach.
Stillness is the only thing worth mastering in this life,

and when you do,
the reward is not in the butterfly
landing on your skin,
but in a joy so overwhelming,
you won't even notice when she goes.

An Ongoing List of My Son's First Words When He Wakes

Today is my favorite day.
The sun has been awake for hours.
Do you think it will rain?
Will the orange trees complain?
I can't wait to go to school.
Do I have to go to school?
Where did my tooth go?
Where did my sock go?
Where did you go?
Can I have paper?
I need to make a list.
Who takes care of the plants?
Who do the plants take care of?
What about the windows, who cleans those?
Do you think the squirrels will visit us again?
What if we didn't do anything today?
What if we didn't go anywhere today?
What if we just stayed in this bed?
I had the craziest dream,
but I can't remember what it was,
or if you were there,
or if I was there, either.
Do you know that the sun is shining
even though you can't see it
through the clouds.
I know, because I've been up there.

An Ongoing List of My Son's First Words When He Wakes

Today is my favorite day.
The sun has been awake for hours.
Do you think it will rain?
will the orange trees complain?
I can't wait to go to school.
Do I have to go to school?
Where did my tooth go?
Where did my sock go?
Where did you go?
Can I have paper?
I need to make a list.
Who takes care of the plants?
Who do the plants take care of?
What about the windows, who cleans those?
Do you think the squirrels will visit us again?
What if we didn't do anything today?
What if we didn't go anywhere today?
What if we just stayed in this bed?
I had the craziest dream,
but I can't remember what it was,
or if you were there,
or if I was there, either.
Do you know that the sun is shining
even though you can't see it
through the clouds.
I know, because I've been up there.

The Hurt You Give

You cannot know this yet, but you—
Yes, you, all rolls and coos and cotton sleeves—
you will be the one to do the hurting in this world.
It feels impossible, I know,
that something so soft
could cause another to bleed,
but you will become vicious.

Venom will drip from your lips
into the veins of those you love,
and you, sweet soul, will wound.
But when you do, remember,
you are more than the hurt you give.
Purpose lives behind the walls of grief,
inside the places where pain seeks to hide.

Yes, your world right now is light blues
and tender whispers,
and delicate curls they've yet to cut
from a head that has never ached.
When this ferocity finds you,
and anger engulfs you,
embrace it without hesitation.

You cannot, you will not
shut it out, or cut it off,
or deny this pulsing part of you
that will push them into their completeness.
Allow yourself to go dark,
even darker still, my dear,
until darkness becomes all there is.

They cannot know this yet, but you—
Yes, you, with weary eyes and weathered hands—
you will be the one to do the healing in this world.
It feels impossible, I know
but you are forging the path
that helps guide them back
to the light.

The Hurt You Give

You cannot know this yet, but you—
Yes, you, all rolls and coos and cotton sleeves—
you will be the one to do the hurting in this world.
It feels impossible, I know,
that something so soft
could cause another to bleed,
but you will become vicious.

Venom will drip from your lips
into the veins of those you love,
and you, sweet soul, will wound.
But when you do, remember,
you are more than the hurt you give.
Purpose lives behind the walls of grief,
inside the places where pain seeks to hide.

Yes, your world right now is light blues
and tender whispers,
and delicate curls they've yet to cut
from a head that has never ached.
When this ferocity finds you,
and anger engulfs you,
embrace it without hesitation.

You cannot, **you will** not
shut it out, or cut it off,
or deny this pul**sing** part of you
that will push them **into the**ir completeness.
Allow yourself to go dark,
even darker still,
until **darkness** becomes all there is.

They cannot know this yet, but you—
Yes, you, with weary eyes and weathered hands—
you will be the one to do the healing in this world.
It feels impossible, I know
but you are forging the path
that helps guide them back
to the light.

BURN

Part of You

This is the beginning of sadness.
When you see your mother
as something separate from you,
no longer another limb, but the truth.
She is a shadow,
steadily stepping further away.

All of your cells once formed
from hers have divided.
Your universe expands while
your understanding constricts.
Until today, everything
has been an extension,
its existence tethered to your own.

But now you see
your mother leaving,
breathing away from you.
She becomes something-not-you,
entirely another, and you are not of her.

She is a new creature
that feeds and bleeds and feels
while you become a witness
to this tragic transition.
If only it were just her—
but everywhere you look,
this realization follows.

If your mother is your mother,
then that flower is a flower.
That cloud, a cloud.
That horse, a horse.
That sun, a sun.
That river, a river.

You are you
and yours is now a world
where everything is isolated,
entities parsed, separation all around.

But look closer,
until you've found the truth.
The flower is the sun,
the river is the horse,
Your mother is the cloud.
Remember that when they ask:
who are you?

Part of You

This is the beginning of sadness.
When you see your mother
as something separate from you,
no longer another limb, but the truth
She is a shadow,
steadily stepping further away.

All of your cells once formed
from hers have divided.
Your universe expands while
your understanding constricts.
Until today, everything
has been an extension,
its existence tethered to your own.

But now you see
your mother leaving,
breathing away from you.
She becomes something not you:
entirely another, and you are not of her.

She is a new creature
that feeds and bleeds and feels
while you become a witness
to this tragic transition.
If only it were just her -
but everywhere you look,
this realization follows.

If your mother is your mother,
then that flower is **a flower**.
That cloud, **a cloud**.
That horse, **a horse**.
That sun, **a sun**.
That river, **a river**.

You are you
and yours is now a world
where **everything** is isolated,
entities parsed, separation all around.

But look closer,
until you've found the truth
The flower is the sun,
the river is the horse,
Your mother is the cloud
Remember that when they ask:
who are you?

Toward Perfection

Some days you are the sand
and I am the Hag Stone
you're grinding toward perfection.

We found them on your beach,
the one where we'd go to argue,
the one where we'd go to reconnect,
your hand resting on mine
the entire drive there,
the entire drive home.

They say these stones stay hidden,
deciding when they're ready to be seen;
and in that instant, they seek you out.
They're meant to ward off witches,
illness, and the inevitable—

You wear your stone around your neck
a thick thread holding it in place.
I set my stone on my desk beside the vase
you fill with flowers from the little stand
tucked on the side of our winding road.

Somedays I am the sand
and you are the Hag Stone
I'm polishing toward perfection.

Toward Perfection

Some days you are the sand
and I am the Hag Stone
you're grinding toward perfection.

We found them on your beach,
the one where we'd go to argue,
the one where we'd go to reconnect,
your hand resting on mine
the entire drive there,
the entire drive home.

They say these stones stay hidden,
deciding when they're ready to be seen;
and in that instant, they seek you out.
They're meant to ward off witches,
illness, and the inevitable—

You wear your stone around your neck
a thick thread holding it in place.
I set my stone on my desk beside the vase
you fill with flowers from the little stand
tucked on the side of our winding road.

Somedays I am the sand
and you are the Hag Stone
I'm polishing toward perfection.

You Already Are

I ask about your childhood
and you tell me instead about pain
dragged around like a corpse
for the last twenty, thirty, forty years.

This is how it often goes,
start from the beginning
scratch tally marks on the walls
counting up your parents' flaws.
Catalogue their failings alphabetically—
abusive, belligerent, catatonically depressed.

I watch you leave out
what they were asked to give up,
forced to survive,
how despite not wanting to live
they somehow kept you alive.
You erase all their hurt in the writing of your own
because no one wants to read that side of the story.
A monster can only stay a monster
if they're never brought into the light.

I ask about your scars
still tender after all this time
You insist they're kept as evidence without
realizing they've become more like a locket
hanging around your neck.
Suffering is your inheritance,
the only connection to them you have left.

I ask about forgiveness
and you tell me instead about deserving
You highlight their hatred,
their ignorance, their judgement.
in the stories that you choose to tell
and the stories you choose to ignore.
I read between the lines you refuse to bury
because you're still reaching for their love.
You tell me how you'll never ever be like them
without ever seeing how like them you already are.

You Already Are

I ask about **your** childhood
and you tell me instead about pain
dragged around like a corpse
for the last twenty, thirty, forty years.

This is how it often goes,
start from the beginning
scratch tally marks on the walls
counting up your **parents'** flaws.
Catalogue their failings alphabetically—
abusive, belligerent, catatonically depressed.

I watch you leave out
what they were asked to **give** up,
forced to survive,
how despite not wanting to live
they somehow kept **you** alive.
You erase **all** their hurt in the writing of your own
because no one wants to read that side of the story.
A monster can only stay a monster
if **they**'re never brought into the light.

I ask about your scars
still tender after all this time
You insist they're kept as evidence without
realizing they've become more like a locket
hanging around your neck.
Suffering is your inheritance,
the only connection to them you **have left**.

I ask about **forgive**ness
and you tell me instead about deserving
You highlight their hatred,
their ignorance, their judgement.
in the stories that you choose to tell
and the stories you choose to ignore.
I read between the lines you refuse to bury
because you're still reaching for their love.
You tell me how you'll never ever be like **them**
without ever seeing how like them you already are.

Grace

I will not be unkind to you.

Not because you deserve

my kindness, my softness, my grace

but solely because you cross my path.

The sun does not choose whom to warm

nor whom to deny its embrace.

If you stand in the way of light,

it will shine on you just the same.

Grace

I will not be unkind to you.

Not **be**cause you deserve

my kindness, my softness, my grace

but solely because you cross my path.

The sun does not choose who to warm

nor whom to deny its embrace.

If you st**a**nd in the way of **light**,

it will shine on you just the same.

Less Than Sin

I caught a rat on a sticky trap,
hidden under the hood of my car.
A horrible thing to do, I know—
and somehow still,
not the worst I've done.

I blame it on the sound
from behind the dash:
little claws on coils,
him climbing about the engine,
pawing new paths,
running rampant along wires,
gnawing through seatbelts,
nesting in the hollow of the spare tire.

I didn't want him to die,
I just wanted him gone.
I knew when I saw him
how wrong it was—
still twitching, breath quickening,
pure panic.
I waited with him while he died,
sitting quietly by his side,
so he wouldn't be alone.

When he finally stopped fighting,
I couldn't remember
why I'd been so resistant
to his existence.
I placed him there on the gravel,
because I didn't want to touch death.
And because I was curious to see
what might happen
once death touched him.

First came the flies,
and then came the maggots,
while the ants hurried
to form a thick, blotted line.
They picked at him in orderly chaos,
for days it went like this—
tugging out hair,
excavating the eyes and ears,
disappearing him from the inside out.

The colony fed and fed,
bringing bites back
to their home in the hollow trees.

Each day I went out
to see as his body bloated,
and deflated, and flattened.
The ants outdid themselves
until all that remained were
dry bones and matted fur
and a brown smudge
where the peanut butter had been.

What nature had done
was not a cruelty.
What I had done was:
a trick, a trap,
whether sticky or snap, or shock.
I lured him into a place, and put him
where I knew he'd never survive,
using something that I knew he liked.
That kind of manipulation
is nothing less than sin.

Less Than Sin

I caught a rat on a sticky trap,
hidden under the hood of my car.
A horrible thing to do, I know—
and somehow still,
not the worst I've done.

I blame it on the sound
from behind the dash:
little claws on coils,
him climbing about the engine,
pawing new paths,
running rampant along wires,
gnawing through seatbelts,
nesting in the hollow of the spare tire.

I didn't want him to die,
I just wanted him gone.
I knew when I saw him
how wrong it was—
still twitching, breath quickening,
pure panic.
I waited with him while he died,
sitting quietly by his side,
so he wouldn't be alone.

When he finally stopped fighting,
I couldn't remember
why I'd been so resistant
to his existence.
I placed him there on the gravel,
because I didn't want to touch death.
And because I was curious to see
what might happen
once death touched him.

First came the flies,
and then came the maggots,
while the ants hurried
to form a thick, blotted line.
They **pick**ed at him in orderly chaos,
for days it went like this—
tugging out hair,
excavating the eyes and ears,
disappearing him from the inside out.

The colony fed and fed, bringing bites back
to their ho**me** in the hollow trees.

Each day I went out
to see as his body bloated,
and deflated, and flattened.
T**he** ants out**did** themselves
until all that remained were
dry bones and matted fur
and a brown smudge
where the peanut butter had been.

What nature had done
was not **a cruel**ty.
What I had done was:
a trick, a **trap**.
whether sticky or snap, or shock.
I lured him into a place, and **put** him
where I knew he'd never survive,
using something that I knew he liked.
That kind of manipulation
is nothing less than s**in**.

Orbiting Betrayal

You asked
...how many times
must I
forgive you
and I said
...how many times
must I
apologize

Healing

My hurt
doesn't feel
like hurt
in your hands,
it feels like
the first grasps
of healing.

Before

I know what happened to my body
that night you turned my memory off.

The bones are branded by
all that the mind can bury.

I knew it when I woke up,
warm cheek on cold concrete,
cigarette ashes on the sink,
Sharpie on the back of the bathroom stall.

I knew it when I keyed the ignition,
hands shaking
windows down
crying through red lights
not slowing, not stopping.

I knew it when I took off the dress
you said you liked,
before you bought me the drink
you said I'd like.

I knew it when I lowered
into the tub and felt—
the burn of where you'd been,
without my permission,
without my knowing.

What does it feel like
to rob a house when no one is home?
What does it feel like
to steal something unopened?
What does it feel like
to leave fingerprints without worry?

You knew you would never be caught
because the police would never be called.
You would go free while I refused to bear
what happened to my body
that night you turned my memory off.

When I put my head under water
and screamed like the drowning do,
I knew I would create
a counterfeit memory.

With darkness as my witness,
I crafted a lie to survive the truth—
I filled in the blanks, rewriting
the life you took with you.

That night,
I went to the bar.
I danced.
I had one drink.
I came home.
The locks were still on.
Nothing out of place.
Everything exactly as I'd left it.

And still, the shadow of you
consumed me.
And when the man who loved me
touched me,
I reminded and reminded
and reminded my skin
that we do not remember you.

I always knew
I'd exhume you
the second I was ready—
but not a moment before.

So Close

We hiked down to a place
where no one could hear us scream.
We let our throats open the sky,
unsteady the earth,
shake rock out of place.

This is what it sounds like
to release held breath,
held hope, held pain—
guttural, growling, hungry.

A scream like this invites tears,
something opens,
something awakens,
something alive from infancy,
a longing for a comfort so far away
no metric can measure the distance.

You have been giving less and less
of yourself to us for some time,
and I have been lying to us both—
pretending I can survive on so little.
You walk ahead of me and I see
something between us has broken and we
have never fixed anything so fragile before.

You stopped, lifting your nose
in the air that had turned with rot
we circled until we found her there,
under the shade of a cottonwood,
belly bloated, hair matted,
flies colonizing her sockets.

We covered our mouths and studied her,
this great beast looking as though
she were only resting
in her favorite spot,
her back casually turned to the sun.

We once saw a herd of them
feeding along the cliffs in Big Sur.
You said, 'Look at them,
they don't know how lucky they are,
these cows have the best view in the world.'
We were so close then.

We made up the story,
of how she'd died of thirst,
her body drying from the inside out,
only half a mile from a creek
running wild with water.
'She was so close,' you said,
taking my hand in yours.

Together, we hiked back up to the place
where no one would hear us scream.
We watched the sky close,
the earth steady,
rock settle back into place.

Stop Running Away

That earwig is **not** a scorpion;
That bask shark is **not** a great white;
That leatherleaf fern is **not** bracken;
That black bear is **not** a grizzly;
That lynx is **not** a cougar.

That blackberry bush is **not** poison oak;
That redback is **not** a black widow;
That gopher snake is **not** a rattler;
That sand dollar is **not** a sea urchin;
That hoverfly is **not** a wasp.

That blueberry is **not** a nightshade;
That skate is **not** a stingray;
That swallow is **not** a bat;
And forgiveness is **not** weakness.

These are **t h i n g s** you'll learn
when you **s t o p** running away.

Hawks

Don't mistake
the writing of birds
as ignorance,
as if I do not know
what our world has become.
It is because
of what our world has become
that I am lifting my eyes
toward heaven.

EMBERS

Come

You
without love
for me
are like a house
with the lights
shut off
empty
abandoned
an eviction notice yellowing
on the front door
boarded windows
with wooden edges
blackening
grass overgrown
berry bushes
once picked bare
now bow down
to the patches of lawn
scorched, the sycamore
surrendered
to the sun.

I
without love
for you
am driving
out of my way
into our past
every house
that wasn't ours
stands defiant
still radiating
with life
I slow
at the stop sign
lower the window
and throw wildflower seeds
unable to accept
what we've become.

Thank You, Five.

Sometimes it feels
like we're all performing life,
and aren't we?
Both the audience
and the actor.

You, center stage,
you play the victim.
You, with the strong jaw,
you play the villain.

You shuffle around off to the side,
look busy, unbearably busy,
fidgeting, fidgeting, fixing nothing.
And you, just sit there and look pretty.

The rest of you pace offstage
until you're called.
Don't break character.
Don't turn your back to the audience.
Don't mumble.
Throw your voice, reach the balcony.

Play it up—
give me urgency,
give me ecstasy,
give me tension.

Now beg him;
he's leaving you,
he's never coming back.

Cry, dammit, cry real tears.
Perfect, now strike her,
mean it,
but don't leave a mark.

We need more blood.
We need more emotion.
We need more time.

Make it raw.
Make it relatable,
make it original.

Don't improvise,
stick to your script.
There, yes, yes, you have it.
They believe you—
You believe you.

Close

You will try to find me
in the body
of every other woman
you enter.

You will search for me
in her words,
but find everything
written in reverse.

You will try to mold her
into the outline I left behind,
but find she is not enough
to fill the bedsheet of my ghost.

Do not punish her.
Do not cool the air
when you pull away your warmth.
Do not drain her with your longing.

Let her be
the beginning
of a different story
with a shorter ending.

Our book, now in ashes,
will rest in an urn
in the room you will never
give her the key to.

Try and love her,
but do not make her suffer
for her one
and only sin—

the appeal of her
and the repel of her,
which is that she is not me,
not even close.

Your Own Breath

Stop searching
beyond your own skin
for answers to the questions
that linger within you.

There is no map,
no how-to or prescription,
that can unveil the truths
you hold safely within your ribs.

It would be like asking
a bear about winter.
He would tell you
only of warmth,
and solitude,
and a full belly slowly shrinking.

What does a hibernator know
of snow's cold kiss,
from his snug den,
sinking and rising
into the land of torpor?

It would be like asking
a penguin about winter,
only to hear about
the heat of a huddle,
the comfort of community,
the feeling of a fragile shell
between his feet.

It would be like asking
a flamingo about winter,
she'd speak of skies tinted by sun
soaring to lands where lakes await
with a buffet of shrimp and algae
where waters never freeze
and feathers stay vibrant
through to spring.

There is no one,
no matter their experience,
who can guide you better
than your own breath—

Trust the compass
you were born with,
buried deep within your chest,
waiting and waiting and waiting
to be opened.

Only One Answer

My son strings beads
of devastating questions
through me before bed.

"If there was a train coming and you had to choose
to save me or save Daddy,
who would you—"

—You.

His eyes, all white;
His mouth, all O;
His mother, suddenly,
a murderer.

"If the house was on fire and you had to choose
to save me or our puppy,
who would you—"

—You.

"If the boat was sinking and you had to choose
me or the president,
who would you—"

—You.

"If the plane was crashing, and you had to choose,
me or Aya,
who would you—"

—You.

"If a Meteor was coming and you had to choose,
me or everyone else in the world,
who would you—"

—You

"If only one of us could survive and you had to choose,
me or you,
who would you—"

—You.

The answer will never be
anything other than you.
The word will never come out
of my mouth less certain,
less immediate, less unapologetic.

This is all motherhood gives you—
one answer, to every unthinkable question.

Bounty

I worship in the church of Flora,
bending my knees in grassy pews
as I pray to sunflowers.

I pluck petals,
reciting their wisdom in verses:
ask, receive, ask, receive.

I plant seeds as a practice of gratitude,
my basket fills with thank-yous.
Frangipani and Jasmine surrender themselves
falling to the ground, still fragrant.

And into my life, I bring these gifts:
their scents, their sentiments, their truths.
I have seen too much beauty in our world
to believe that it's all barren shadow.

I've seen beauty lining sidewalks,
flourishing in endless fields,
spreading over rigid lines meant to divide us,
sprouting from rock, stretching veins of survival.

A world without flowers is not
a world in which I wish to exist.
Burn me in a bed of marigolds,
heaven-bound with bounty.

How to Waste a Life

Hold on to what hurts;
cling to disappointments like limpets
that decorate tide-swept stones.
Let no hand, however gentle,
pry you from your rock of fury
for without it, you might
drown in contentment.

Follow each betrayal into the deep,
grab it by the tail,
and let it drag you to the ocean's bed,
rolling the breath from your being.

Deny forgiveness, hoard it
as the octopus does
with the senseless treasures she steals.
Gather up your grievances like sea glass,
believing its weight might anchor you.

Refuse any balm of kindness,
as though your salvation lies
not in the letting go,
but in the relentless grip
of what you cannot
will not
release.

Flow Forward

The past is a thief
and you willingly
turn out your pockets to him.
Take my laughter, take my ease, take my peace.

You plead, hands raised, before you
unbuckle, unclasp, unload
everything you've ever cherished
into his greedy palms.

You are left without psalms,
only shadows, stale resentments,
dead horses—twice beaten.
Nothing will change what's happened here.

And yet, you give years
of your life
to the lure of
rewriting.

What if
I had?
What if
we had?

Do not convince yourself
that anything was meant
to be different.

Nature does not do this;
she does not cling.
The ground consumes
what has fallen.

Even birds know
to build nests for one season.
They understand what you still don't:
There is grace found in releasing.

No creature lingers in this river of hope but you.
In defiance, you build a boat
and float as far as the current
can take a person, a pebble, a past.

Nature remains indifferent to loss,
while your fixation costs you everything.
Watch the water; she will teach you
how to flow forward.

Orbiting Goodbye

I asked
...how many times
must you
let me go
and he said
...how many times
must you
keep on coming back

She Doesn't Erase

They say grief is love with nowhere to go,
but I know better.

Grief is love that lost her way—
love with a destination, but no map.

Grief is love sitting at your feet,
waiting to be picked up, carried home.

Grief is love slipping back in without knocking,
asking to hear once more
that what we had was real.

It is ours, and nothing
can take that away—
not even the detour or distraction of pain.

Grief is not the slamming door,
but the click of unlocking.

Grief is love drawing, love singing,
love reclaiming her place.

But one thing grief will never do—
she doesn't erase.

ASHES

More

All of the love
I've ever given
has turned
to smoke

More

All of the love
I've ever **give**n
has turned
to s**mok**e

If You Loved Me
You Would Know

I used to believe
that if you loved me
you would know
the contours of my pain
and in that knowing
you'd steer your touch away from
those places I'd mapped
so thoroughly for you to avoid
here, here and especially here
so as not to awaken
the little ghosts that have made their beds
in the curves of my scars
but there you are, brushing your thumb
against every hurt that existed before you.

If You Loved Me
You Would Know

I used to believe
that if you loved me
you would know
the contours of my pain
and in **that** knowing
you'd steer your touch away from
those places I'd mapped
so thoroughly for you to avoid
here, here and especially here
so as not to awaken
the little ghosts that have made their beds
in the curves of my scars
but there you are, brushing your thumb
against every hurt that existed before you.

Pray

Before you bow
to the calling of death,
I pray you witness in wonder
as your blueprints come to life.

I pray you study the flattened dirt
and envision what beauty could blossom there.
Imagine a family, not yet formed,
leaving footprints in time.

I pray you pay attention to the progress of each day
that you witness the moon as she swallows the sun
over the slow-motion construction of a house
and the even slower-motion construction of a home.

I pray you listen patiently
to the sounds of this symphony,
a chorus of workers waiting as beeping cranes back up,
the tumbling bass echoing off rocks dropped on rocks.

I pray you plant only what you'll pick,
that you build a treehouse for the kids
and the grandkids, and remember even you
will yearn for a space to share secrets.

I pray you spend weeks choosing
locks for the children's doors
but give years learning
how to keep them open.

I pray you accept
the endless time it takes
to decide on lights, and knobs,
and identical shades
named beige, stone, sand.

I pray you know
that the decision to marry you
under the oak tree, in the spring
only took a moment.

I pray you cherish
the making of what you have made.
So much light coming in,
so much light going out.

I pray you bow
to the life
being witnessed
by these walls.

Pray

Before you bow
to the calling of death,
I pray you witness in wonder
as **your** blueprints come to life.

I pray you study the flattened dirt
and en**vision** what beauty could blossom there.
Imagine a family, not yet formed,
leaving footprints in time.

I pray you pay attention to the progress of each day
that you w**i**tne**s**s the moon as she swallows the sun
over the slow-motion construction of a house
and the even slower-motion construction of a home.

I pray you listen **patiently**
to the sounds of this symphony,
a chorus of workers **waiting** as beeping cranes back up,
the tumbling bass echoing off rocks dropped on rocks.

I pray you plant only what you'll pick,
that you build a treehouse **for** the kids
and the grandkids, and remember even **you**
will yearn for a space **to** share secrets.

I pray you spend weeks choosing
locks for the children's doors
but give years **learning**
how to keep them open.

I **pray** you accept
the endless time it takes
to decide on lights, and knobs,
and identical shades
named beige, stone, sand.

I pray you know
that the decision to marry you
under the oak tree, in the spring
only took a moment.

I pray you cherish
the making of what you have made.
So much light coming in,
so much light going out.

I pray you bow
to the life
being witnessed
by these walls.

You're Missing It

You are as tormented as the persimmons,
waiting the entirety of fall,
to ripen from green to amber to zest.

You are finally pulled from your rest between branches
but forever too bitter
to be bitten into.

You will become bird food, and the bird
will become fox food, and the fox
will become chase for the bobcats.

You are always waiting for something less ordinary,
and through the haze of impatience,
you've yet to set eyes on the extraordinary that's arrived.

You stayed inside your room
when you were a boy, for hours, for days,
through the entire faucet-drip of childhood.

You kept only the company locked in that beautiful head
of yours, whose scars I'll trace with fingertips,
when I shave you down to skin one afternoon.

You have always lived in an endless realm of possibility
and because so much is possible,
you keep seeking, refusing to accept what is.

You leave the rest of us wondering where it is you go
when your eyes close and you allow yourself
to float further away from where we are.

And that far place is where you've stayed
all this time I've been following behind you shouting:
You're missing it, you're missing it, you're missing it.

You're Missing It

You are as tormented as the persimmons,
waiting the entirety of fall,
to ripen from green to amber to zest.

You are finally pulled from your rest between branches
but forever too bitter
to be bitten into.

You **will** become bird food, and the bird
will become fox food, and the fox
 will become **chase** for the bobcats.

You are always waiting for something less ordinary,
and through the haze of impatience,
you've yet to set eyes on **the** extra**ordinary** that's arrived.

You stayed inside your room
when you were a boy, for hours, for **days**,
through the entire faucet-drip of childhood.

You kept only the company locked in **that** beautiful head
of **you**rs, whose scars I'll **t**race with fingertips,
when I shave you down to skin one afternoon.

You have always lived in an endless realm of possibility
and because so much is possible,
you keep seeking, refusing **to** accept what is.

You **leave** the rest of us wondering where it is you go
when your eyes close and you allow yourself
to float further away from where we are.

And that far place is where you've stayed
all this time I've been following **behind** you shouting:

You're missing it, you're missing it, you're missing it.

My Love

I beg you—
please
don't get lost
in the story
you're writing
about your life.

Your past is a book
that can be closed,
placed back on the shelf.

Leave the horrors,
the cliffhangers,
the chaos
where they are.

Come back to bed
beside me—
your leg resting on mine,
under covers where everything
is still alive,
not yet penned
to the page.

Ours

You asked me to write your eulogy
while we were still alive.
I thought it strange to ask
not a friend nor mistress nor wife
for postmortem praise.

What was I to you in those days when
we witnessed sunrise and sunset from bed,
worshipping one another,
tracing out treasure maps
with fingertips and lips,
our tongues tasting sweat, wetting ribs,
you guiding rhythm with gripped hips—
What am I to you now, my love?

Maybe this was another one of your tests,
to see if I saw you as you saw yourself.
Maybe it was a test to see if I saw you at all.
I once asked, 'Who in this world really knows you?'
You named me just after your mother.
How terrifying only to be known
by the women you desperately fear you might lose.
Who will know you after we're gone?

At your funeral, they'll say,
'To know him was to love him.'
But that torches truth—
it was only after you left us
that I clearly saw
the mosaic of contradiction
you were made of.

You will be memorialized with praise.
Through tears, they will say
what a beautiful father you were,
what a generous man you were,
what brilliance, what genius,
what courage and conviction—
and they will not be wrong.

If you were a painting, and you were—
In loving you, I saw the Recto,
in losing you, I saw the Verso.
And so, I will write of the well-hidden
Impasto of you, the layers beneath.

You were both the fire and the burn,
how your love could warm or blister.
I will tell how you loved like a storm-worn cliff—
the view unimaginable, the fall inevitable.

I witnessed your magic long enough
to slip out of its spell.
With one sentence you could convince me
I was capable of soaring over impossibilities,
and with your next breath
you could render me utterly useless,
a blank sheet of a person, undeserving
of faith, of fidelity, of forgiveness.

I loved you even though,
you set towering standards
for yourself and me, leaving us
no choice but to feel as though we were
always, always, failing, falling, breaking.

I loved you, even though
you were a merciless teacher,
all of the tenderness laid like bricks,
once solid but could so quickly
crumble with only a look of disappointment
a look I grew to know well.

I loved you, even though
you earned my loyalty
by holding me so unfailingly soft
before scolding in your unmistakable tone:
Life was never meant to be a cradle.
Vulnerability was the ultimate luxury,
one of the few things you could not afford.

To lose you was to feel the absence of a roof
in a room swept into chaos by unrelenting wind.
The first day without you, I walked through town,
pulling my shoulders in, disappearing myself,
shuddering at the realization
I was no longer under your protection.

You are gone and the world
stretches out before me,
asking, 'What will we do
with all of this stopped love?'

Our memories are the balm
and the burden and I
don't dare deny them space and grace
to live beside me,
warming your half of the bed,
reminding me what we were,
what we are to one another.

You asked me to write your eulogy,
so here it is, my love:
You were the tempest and the calm,
the lesson and the reward.
The casket doesn't know
how many bodies go down with it,
so my bones will lay there,
eternally hopeful,
right beside yours.

Not only a Touch

You are there
in the deepest part of me,
unforgotten.
A song on repeat, its chorus
gripping my throat.
A poem I wrote
on the palm of my hand
so it could never leave me.

But you will.
And when you do,
I'll watch as you
find yourself
over and over,
in as many ways as life allows you
to unearth the treasures
and the bones we buried.

Do not mourn me
and I will not mourn you.
Let life echo memories
of the drawing you once made
that hung on the wall of our home
the caption lit by the window's
kaleidoscope: *Happiness happens
when the light touches you.*

Not only a Touch

You are there
in the deepest part of me,
unforgotten.
A song on repeat, its chorus
gripping my throat.
A poem I wrote
on the palm of my hand
so it could never leave me.

But you will.
And when you do,
I'll watch as you
find yourself
over and over,
in as many ways as life allows you
to unearth the treasures
and the bones we buried.

Do not mourn me
and I will not mourn you.
Let life echo memories
of the drawing you once made
that hung on the wall of our home
the caption lit by the window's
kaleidoscope: *Happiness happens
when the light touches you.*

Press Between Pages

My grandfather is dying,
and outside the hospital, a man sells mangoes
with limón y sal. My aunt and I split one;
we both like what's bitter.
She walks under the shade of a guayacán,
and white florets fall into her hair.
I tell her, *wait, don't move,*
we want them to stay.

My grandfather is dying,
and every day we come and say goodbye,
we can only visit two at a time—
these are the rules for the final hours.
So we lick salt from our fingers, sign in, and wait
in the chapel's pews outside his room.
Rosaries hang beside the candles
we are not allowed to light.

My grandfather is dying,
and his chest heaves
while the machine beside him sings
its constant song: still alive, still alive, still alive.
My aunt lifts his hand to her face
and cries into his palm, asking forgiveness,
offering forgiveness, while
her white florets fall onto his sheets.

My grandfather is dying,
and I hold his one hand with my two.
I don't think he'd ever felt my fingers
brushing his, not since
I was a girl and he was guiding me
through church, sitting me in the front row
reserved for the pastor's kids.
Why do we do, during death,
the things we refuse to do in life?
Soften, whisper, apologize.

My grandfather is dying,
and my mother paces in the
corridor, praying for a miracle
but there is no supplication to delay death,
no coercing her to skip this soul,
move on to the next house.
But if there were—
it would sound something like,
pleasepleasepleaseplease.

My grandfather is dying,
and dying and dying
and we are slowly realizing
that this miracle has already
come and left,
the miracle that he lived,
that any of us get to live at all.

My grandfather is gone,
and when they tell us
we hold one another and weep
from sorrow and relief.
No one knows the heaviness of hope
until it has burrowed into your bones—
unrelenting, gnawing, digging.

My grandfather is gone,
and no one asked me to go in,
but my mother has gone,
and my aunt has gone,
and they are teaching me
how to lose a father,
a lesson I don't want to need.

My grandfather is gone,
and the doctor leads us through a maze
to the hidden hospital basement,
where the bodies go.
I stand at his feet, his belly swollen
so I couldn't see his face, but I imagine
the look of someone seeing the truth,
still etched on his cheeks.

My grandfather is gone,
and as they gently slip a tag
around his ankle
I think of when my son was born
how I kept that tag
when we left the hospital
and pressed it in a baby book
between clips of hair and his footprint—
how fast this all goes.
I watch as they zip closed the black canvas
and lift him from one bed to another.

My grandfather is gone,
and I have never been so close to the ending,
touching death before it was sanitized.
My mother, my aunts, my grandmother,
we walk beside the stretcher,
exiting behind the hospital where a white van waits,
its doors already open as if welcoming him
through heaven's gates.

My grandfather is gone,
and we watch two men load his body,
shut the doors, and double-tap the window.
The van disappears into traffic, behind
taxis, motos and chivas.

We let go of him the same way
as all of the other grandfathers,
absent fathers, never-were-fathers
homeless men, and holy men.
I want to take a piece of him
but there is nothing left.

So I reach for a lowered branch and pocket
a palm of florecillos to press between pages.

My grandfather is gone,
and buses fill with people
coming to honor him, bury him,
thank him goodbye.

We wail and we laugh, we sing, we kiss,
we send white balloons to the sky
and throw red roses into the same earth
that will one day widen her floorboards
and invite us all to join him.

This thought sits perched on my shoulder
chirping, both reminder and relief.

Carrying You Home

You are seven, eyes wide,
breath strawberry mint,
in footed flannel pajamas.
And you ask,
Will it hurt, Mama?

Will it hurt
When death comes
to take me?

I've never lied to you,
and refuse to start now
in this moment,
on this bed,
with your trusting head against
my heart—

Yes, I tell you, gently.
Yes, it will hurt.
It will be an unbearable ache,
a cut that never heals over,
a wound forever pulsing,

Yes, my love, it will hurt...
for every single
person who is left
here to grieve you.

But you,
my little king,
you will not hurt—
you will be flying.

The sky will open
and soften from midnight
into morning's vast glow,
ready to welcome you
with the sparrows
and starlings,
carrying you home.

Surrender

We saw a dead hummingbird on my birthday.
She lay on the ground, still and serene,
surrounded by catkins.

It was as if the willow tree witnessed this loss
and did what little he could
to bury her with honor.

That night, as I fell asleep
with your sweet breath on my neck,
I asked my life, *what can we let go of?*

Then watched as my grip loosened
on every single thing I thought
I could never surrender.

Surrender

We saw a dead hummingbird on my birthday.
She lay on the ground, still and serene,
surrounded by catkins.

It was as if the willow tree witnessed this loss
and did what little he could
to bury her with honor.

That night, as I fell asleep
with your sweet breath on my neck,
I asked my life, *what can we let go of?*

Then watched as my grip loosened
on every single thing I thought
I could never surrender.

Burn After Reading

Nature, after fire, is defiant:
whatever disaster transpired
can never define her.
She is your reminder:
after blossoms are swallowed
up in neon flames,
after smoke clears,
beneath charred remains,
in embers, she still breathes.

Her soil, turned to ash,
scatters in the wind,
her story of destruction reaching
and reaching and reaching
those she will never know.
In the morning, she begins again.

She dares anyone who passes by,
not ruthless, not cold, not denying:
Watch me grow.
Watch me blossom.
Watch me burn
even brighter
than ever before.

Burn **After** Reading

Nature, after **fire**, is defiant:
whatever disaster transpired
can never define her.
She is your reminder:
after blossoms are swallowed
up in neon flames,
after smoke clears,
beneath charred **remains**,
in embers, she still breathes.

Her soil, turned to ash,
scatters in the wind,
her story of destruction reaching
and reaching and reaching
those she will never know.
In the morning, she beg**in**s again.

She dares anyone who passes by,
no**t ruth**less, not cold, not denying:
Watch me grow.
Watch me blossom.
Watch me burn
 even brighter
than ever before.

ACKNOWLEDGEMENTS

To you, the reader, thank you for offering your energy, time, and attention my words. These are the most valuable things we have to give one another and I'm honored you chose to share them with me.

This book is a love letter to life. Each of these poems were woven from the threads of the stories I've lived, the voices of those I loved and from every one of you who lent me strength when I could not find my own.

To my teachers, editors, and fellow writers, many of whom started as mentors but became so much more, thank you for leaving me signposts along this path—

Hilton Als, Margot Jefferson, Ben Taylor, Leslie Jamison, Alice Quinn, Rob Spillman, Dan Jones, Reema Zaman, Rivka Galchken, Kate Medina, Mary Bergstrom, Tim Kreider, Elaine Welteroth, Lis Harris, Patricia O'Toole, Arianna Huffington, Margaret Riley King, Elizabeth Gilbert, Adrien LeBlanc, Kate Coyne, Cheryl Strayed, Darin Strauss, Joél Leon, Dani Shapiro, Jess Walter, Ann Patchett, Anne Lamott and Mary Karr— a million thank-yous.

And to the late Mary Oliver, whose quiet encouragement spoke louder than any noise—I wouldn't know poetry the way I do if I hadn't been introduced to it by you.

To the women I have worked with over the years, thank you for trusting me with your stories, and for inviting me to edit your words, knowing I wouldn't leave fingerprints. None of this compares to the joy I get from watching each of you soar. Keep writing.

To Mary Jonitis, who said in our first conversation, "You need to write poetry. Try and give a voice to those without a voice and I don't mean people..."

That call changed everything.

To Zulma, Naomi, Ali, and Adela— when I was ready to heal, you held my hand and walked me to the gate.
I will forever be grateful to each of you.

À Fabrice Penot, mon amour, sans toi, ce livre n'existerait pas. Many of these poems were born from our story, a story that could not have been written any other way. I will always have 'one more thing' to tell you.

To my soulmates: Logan Ford, Nate Timmerman, Clark Henriquez—We've been constants in each other's lives, loving one another through every version of ourselves and allowing each other to shed every veil. Your friendship is one of life's greatest gifts, and I'm incredibly lucky to walk this path with you three. Thank you for always keeping my feet on the ground, not an easy task.

Now, off to the golden helicopter.

A mi familia Henriquez, Perea, Ordoñez—Ustedes son una parte muy importante de quién soy. Gracias por abrirme sus corazones y sus casas, y por recibirme con amor cada vez que volví para sanar. A mi abuelito Carlos, gracias por regalarme tus ojos y tu amor por el arte. A mi abuelita Beatriz, Mama Lita, eres la mujer más fuerte que conozco. Gracias por amarme todos los días de esta vida y de las muchas vidas anteriores. Te adoro.

To my father and my brothers— thank you for teaching me about the quiet kind of love—the kind that warms the car before school, that says, "You look beautiful," when I don't feel beautiful, and that drives 3,000 miles with me so I don't have to do it alone. I love you.

To my mother, Elizabeth. My first classroom was our kitchen table. Thank you for teaching me how to read and write, even when your heart was breaking. You are joy incarnate, and a testament to the power of unconditional love. Thank you for your friendship, your encouragement, and for reading each of these poems as they were being created, singing their praises even if they didn't rhyme.
I am who I am because of you.

And to Noah Rev—my little king. Thank you for choosing me to be your mama in this lifetime. You are the most amazing creature I've ever known—your kindness, your humor, your patience, and your depth. I feel so honored to watch you grow into the man you're becoming. I know I'm not supposed to say this where other people can hear it but baby, you are my best friend. Thank you for letting me share these snippets of our life with the world. The rest will stay unwritten, sacred, locked away in our little safe. Now, what are we going to dream about tonight?

To every person who finds this book, I want you to know that creating this collection has been an absolute joy. I woke up every morning, racing to the page, eager to capture these beautiful snapshots nature gifted me, ready to share the words spirit spoke to me—without fear, without hesitation, without wondering or worrying what comes next.

ABOUT THE AUTHOR

Jessica Ciencin Henriquez is a Colombian-American writer, editor, and teacher. Her writing has been featured in The New York Times, Teen Vogue, Time, Self, Marie Claire, and Oprah, among others. She specializes in literary translation and holds an MFA in Creative Nonfiction from Columbia University.

Driven by her passion for diverse storytelling, Jessica's workshops and courses continue to connect women from across the globe, empowering them to recover their voices and craft their stories with purpose and authenticity. She lives in California with her son.

@thewriterjess

REV PUBLISHING
New York | Los Angeles | Paris | Bogotá

Founded in 2024, we are a boutique literary house committed
to amplifying original voices and transformative stories. Our
carefully curated list includes poetry, memoir, and fiction that
push boundaries and challenge tradition.